CONTENTS

Stories by Maureen Spurgeon

First published 1998
by Brown Watson, England

Reprinted 2001, 2003, 2005, 2007,
2010, 2011, 2013, 2015, 2016, 2017,
2018

ISBN: 978-0-7097-1256-5
© 1998 Brown Watson, England
Printed in Malaysia

Christmas
Stories

Book 2

Brown Watson

ENGLAND

THE LITTLE
CHRISTMAS
TREE

Illustrated by Stephen Holmes

ONCE, on a hill above a town, there was a little Christmas tree. So many big trees grew all around, there was no room for the little tree to spread its roots, so it hardly grew at all. Nobody even knew that the tiny little Christmas tree was even there.

As Christmas time drew near, the
little tree always felt so unhappy.
He could see people looking at
all the other trees and hear the
children laughing and talking to
each other.

"Ooh, look at that lovely big Christmas tree!"
"We can hang lots of presents on those strong branches!"
"This Christmas tree is so nice and tall!"

"Choose me!" thought the little Christmas tree. "Please choose me!" But nobody did. Then, one cold winter's night, something happened. Quite suddenly, a strong wind began to blow.

The wind howled down all the
chimneys, blew under all the
doors and rattled all the
windows. And it whistled through
the branches of all the trees,
tugging hard at the roots.

The little Christmas tree held on for as long as he could. But then a sudden gust of wind blew hard against the bottom branches and he felt himself being lifted high into the air!

"Whoo-Whoo!" whistled the wind, blowing harder than ever. Only one person saw the little Christmas tree whirling and twirling about on that cold, snowy night.

Gradually, the wind died down, as more big, white snowflakes fell from the sky. The little Christmas tree felt himself falling, falling, until he came to rest on a bed of snow.

"About time, too!" came a voice, and a figure in a red cloak and big boots picked up the little Christmas tree. "You always wanted to be a proper Christmas tree, didn't you?"

Little by little, the sky became lighter and a pale sun shone down. "Hey, here's the Christmas tree we wanted!" someone shouted. "Mum said Santa would bring it, Jason!"

"Let's take it indoors," came a boy's voice, "then we'll find a big flower pot or something and fill it with earth. We'll soon have this looking like a real Christmas tree!"

"I'm glad it's a little Christmas
tree!" said Anna. "Big trees need
lots of decorations!"
"And it's tall enough for me to
reach the top branch!" laughed
Jason. "I like it!"

They worked hard all morning,
cutting out paper stars, making
balls of silver foil and hanging
things on all the branches. The
little Christmas tree loved every
minute!

There were lots of games and parties and fun around the little Christmas tree! Someone caught their sleeve on a branch and a small piece broke off. The little Christmas tree tried not to mind.

"Our poor tree!" said Anna.
"All its little green needles are
beginning to fall off."
"That always happens," said
someone else. "Christmas trees
don't last long indoors!"

By the time Christmas was over, the little Christmas tree was very worried. "We'll put the decorations in the cupboard ready for next year!" said Mum. "Any rubbish for the dustmen?"

"What about the little Christmas tree?" asked Jason. "We can't put that in the cupboard."

"No," said Mum, lifting the Christmas tree out of its flower pot. "It will have to go outside."

The poor little Christmas tree trembled so much that a whole shower of green needles fell to the ground. He was taken outside and set down by a cold wall, waiting for the dustmen.

After a while, the little tree was lifted up again – but he hardly cared. All he had ever wanted was to be a real Christmas tree. He had never been so unhappy.

He began to dream that he could hear birds singing, just as they did when he had been with the other trees on the hillside. He thought he heard a voice which sounded just like Jason.

"Look at the birds! They're eating all the food we've put round our tree!" The little Christmas tree looked down at his new, green branches, with the birds darting in and out.

"That little tree has certainly brightened up our back yard!" said Mum.

"YOU always said nothing would grow, because we don't get much sunshine!" said Jason.

"But we really don't WANT our Christmas tree to grow!" said Anna. And all through the months that followed, the birds would come and perch on the tree, chirping and singing.

31

As the days grew shorter, the time came for the birds to fly away to warmer lands. But the little Christmas tree did not mind. Soon, he knew, winter would come once again.

Then he would be a real little
Christmas tree again, with stars
and silver balls. Anna and Jason
loved him. "Because," said Jason,
"we can have a little bit of
Christmas all year round!"

CHRISTMAS
CAROLS, SONGS AND VERSES

Illustrated by Stephen Holmes

WE THREE KINGS OF ORIENT ARE

We three kings of Orient are,
Bearing gifts, we traverse afar-
Field and fountain,
Moor and mountain-
Following yonder star.

CHORUS:

Oh, star of wonder, star of night,
Star of royal beauty bright,
Westward leading, still proceeding,
Guide us to thy perfect light.

THE TWELVE DAYS OF CHRISTMAS

On the first day of Christmas
My true love sent to me
A partridge in a pear tree.

On the second day of Christmas
My true love sent to me
Two turtle doves.

On the third day of Christmas
My true love sent to me
Three French hens.

On the fourth day of Christmas
My true love sent to me
Four calling birds.

On the fifth day of Christmas
My true love sent to me
Five gold rings.

On the sixth day of Christmas
My true love sent to me
Six geese a-laying.

On the seventh day of Christmas
My true love sent to me
Seven swans a-swimming.

On the eighth day of Christmas
My true love sent to me
Eight maids a-milking.

On the ninth day of Christmas
My true love sent to me
Nine drummers drumming.

On the tenth day of Christmas
My true love sent to me
Ten pipers piping.

On the eleventh day of Christmas
My true love sent to me
Eleven ladies dancing.

On the twelfth day of Christmas
My true love sent to me
Twelve lords a-leaping,
Eleven ladies dancing,
Ten pipers piping,
Nine drummers drumming,
Eight maids a-milking,
Seven swans a-swimming,
Six geese a-laying,
Five gold rings,
Four calling birds,
Three French hens,
Two turtle doves
And a partridge in a pear tree.

ONCE IN ROYAL DAVID'S CITY

Once in Royal David's City
Stood a lowly cattle shed,
Where a mother laid her baby
In a manger for His bed;
Mary was that mother mild,
Jesus Christ her little child.

ALL YEAR ROUND

When Spring-time comes,
There's lots to do -
Watching birds and squirrels, too.
Flying kites and pressing flowers,
Now there are more daylight hours.

Summer-time! And, to keep cool,
We play in my big paddling pool!
Picnic lunches, games outside -
Scooters, tricycles to ride.

Autumn now, and all around,
Leaves come fluttering to the ground.
Bonfires, conkers to collect,
And the wild birds to protect.

Winter comes with frost and snow,
We think of someone we all know
Coming down a chimney stack ...
Can you guess what's in his sack?

JINGLE BELLS

Dashing through the snow
In a one horse open sleigh,
O'er the fields we go,
Laughing all the way;
Bells on bob-tail ring,
Making spirits bright,

What fun it is to ride and sing
A sleighing song tonight!
Jingle bells! Jingle bells!
Jingle all the way!
Oh, what fun it is to ride
In a one horse open sleigh!

AWAY IN A MANGER

Away in a manger,
No crib for a bed,
The little Lord Jesus
Laid down His sweet head;

The stars in the bright sky
Look down where He lay,
The little Lord Jesus
Asleep on the hay.

TEDDY'S FAVOURITES

What does a Teddy Bear like best?
Perhaps you'd like to know!
Well...swings and whirly roundabouts
And a bouncy ball to throw...

Currant buns and chocolate,
Honey spread on bread,
And listening to a story,
When I'm tucked up in bed.

Sandcastles! Iced lollipops!
A friendly dog or cat!
Listening to the rain outside
As it goes pitter-pat...

Fireside chats when winter comes...
A gift from Santa Claus...
I think that's all my favourite things.
Can you tell me some of yours?

THE HOLLY AND THE IVY

The holly and the ivy,
When they are both full grown,
Of all the trees that are in the wood,
The holly bears the crown.

CHORUS:
The rising of the sun
And the running of the deer,
The playing of the merry organ,
Sweet singing in the choir.

The holly bears a berry,
As red as any blood,
And Mary bore sweet Jesus Christ
To do poor sinners good.

The holly bears a prickle,
As sharp as any thorn,
And Mary bore sweet Jesus Christ
On Christmas Day in the morn.

The holly bears a bark,
As bitter as any gall,
And Mary bore sweet Jesus Christ
For to redeem us all.

I SAW THREE SHIPS

I saw three ships come sailing in,
On Christmas Day, on Christmas Day,
I saw three ships come sailing in,
On Christmas Day in the morning.

And what was in those ships all three?
On Christmas Day, on Christmas Day,
And what was in those ships all three?
On Christmas Day in the morning.

Our Lord Jesus Christ and his lady,
On Christmas Day, on Christmas Day,
Our Lord Jesus Christ and his lady,
On Christmas Day in the morning.

GOD REST YE MERRY GENTLEMEN

God rest ye merry gentlemen:
Let nothing you dismay.
Remember, Christ our Saviour
Was born on Christmas Day,
To save us all from Satan's power
When we were gone astray.

CHORUS:

Oh, tidings of comfort and joy,
Comfort and joy,
Oh, tidings of comfort and joy!

OH COME, ALL YE FAITHFUL

Oh come, all ye faithful,
Joyful and triumphant,
Oh come ye,
Oh come ye to Bethlehem.
Come and behold Him,
Born the King of Angels

Oh come, let us adore Him,
Oh come, let us adore Him,
Oh come, let us adore Him,
Christ the Lord!

TEDDY'S
CHRISTMAS
PRESENT

Illustrated by Andrew Geeson

Teddy Bear had lots of nice toys.
He had building bricks, a drum, a
scooter, and lots of books and
crayons. But his favourite had
always been Ernest the Engine.
Teddy loved his big, smiley face
and the clickety-clack, clickety-
clack of his wheels, as he pulled
the train behind him.

Ernest had been Teddy's friend
ever since he could remember.
But now, the old engine was
becoming very battered and
worn. More than once, a wheel
had come off and Daddy Bear
had fixed it back on.

His face had become cracked, his buffer beam was bent and his paintwork was scratched. And more than once, his funnel had come off! "I don't know how many more times I can mend Ernest," said Daddy.

"Ernest is getting quite old now, you know," Daddy Bear went on, reaching for his screwdriver. "And you play with him every day, Teddy." "I know," said Teddy sadly. He wondered what he could do.

Just then, Mummy Bear came in,
a shopping basket over her arm.
"What do you think?" she cried.
"Santa Claus is coming to Teddy
Town tomorrow, to see what all
the teddies want for Christmas!"

"Hear that, Teddy?" smiled Daddy.
"You can ask him to bring you a
nice, new engine! You've been a
good bear all year, so I think
Santa Claus would do it."
But Teddy Bear shook his head.

"No," he said, "I don't want a new engine to take the place of Ernest, just because he's old and tired." Then, he thought again. "But I could ask Santa Claus to make him as good as new, couldn't I?"

He sat down to write to Santa Claus that same afternoon, telling him all about Ernest. "I do not want any new toys," he wrote, "but I hope you can make Ernest like new. Please try. Love Teddy."

Santa Claus did not see how he could help. "Toys do get old," he said, stroking his beard. "It's a pity Teddy does not want a new engine. Eric's a nice little one, and he needs a good home . . ."

"All the same" Santa thought, "I know how Teddy feels. I only wish I could make old toys into new ones." A sudden movement of snow caught his eye and he looked across towards the stables.

Dasher had been away having his
hooves trimmed, all ready for
Christmas Eve. Now, he was back
with Dancer, and seeing how glad
both reindeer were to be together
gave Santa Claus an idea!

The teddies of Teddy Town were pleased to see Santa Claus sitting by the big Christmas tree in the market. He soon saw Teddy Bear coming towards him, holding Ernest the engine very tightly.

"So, this is Ernest," he said, in a voice which made Ernest feel very proud. "Yes, I can see why you love him so much, Teddy."

"Can you make him like new again?" asked Teddy.

"Well," said Santa Claus, "I can't make him a new engine on the outside, but I think I can make him a new engine inside. Would that do?" Teddy did not really understand this, but he nodded and smiled.

"As long as I don't have a new engine in place of Ernest," he said. "No, Teddy," Santa Claus laughed, reaching in his sack. "But I do have something so that Ernest will be able to rest a little."

It was a lovely, little engine shed!
Teddy could hardly wait to take it
home and see what Ernest looked
like, resting inside.

"Oh, thank you, Santa Claus!" he
cried. "Thank you very much!"

Teddy put the shed on the floor
and backed Ernest inside.
"There you are, Ernest!" he smiled.
"You have a nice rest, just like
Santa Claus said. You'll soon start
feeling like new."

But, after a while, Teddy became bored just looking at Ernest in the shed. He was sure, too, that the trucks wanted to go round on the rails – if only they had an engine to pull them along!

Teddy felt rather muddled. He did think that Santa Claus had given him a special, magic sort of present to make Ernest feel like new again. Yet, nothing had happened.

But, Teddy was wrong. Being alone in the engine shed had made Ernest think how nice it would be to have a friend. So, he was very pleased when someone in a red cloak and hood put another engine beside him!

"Hello," whispered the new, little engine with a friendly grin.
"My name is Eric!"
"And I'm Ernest!" whispered Ernest.
"Merry Christmas to you, engines!" whispered Santa Claus.

Ernest and Eric talked long into the night, chatting about trains and tracks. It made Ernest feel most important, telling his new friend all about Teddy Bear and the fun they would share.

And what a surprise Teddy had on Christmas morning! It was hard not to like such a bright, cheerful-looking engine, such as Eric – especially when Teddy could see he was already Ernest's friend!

And Ernest? Well, his funnel was still wobbly and his wheels loose, but his smile was bright and his paintwork sparkled. It was plain he felt a new engine inside, just as Santa Claus had promised!

And, as Ernest watched Eric pulling the trucks, Teddy could see that he did not mind having a rest. And how much nicer the shed looked with two engines to go inside! Clever old Santa Claus!

Stories I have read

Christmas on the Farm ☐

Santa's Little Helper ☐

The Christmas Fairy ☐

The Night Before Christmas ☐

Santa's Busy Day ☐